S0-AGG-623

Careers for

TECH GIRLS IN

WEB

DEVELOPMENT

MARYAM WASHINGTON

Rosen
YA™
New York

Published in 2019 by The Rosen Publishing Group, Inc.
29 East 21st Street, New York, NY 10010

Copyright © 2019 by The Rosen Publishing Group, Inc.

First Edition

Library of Congress Cataloging-in-Publication Data

Names: Washington, Maryam, author.
Title: Careers for Tech Girls in Web Development / Maryam Washington.
Description: New York : Rosen Publishing, 2019. | Series: Tech Girls | Includes bibliographical references and index. | Audience: Grades 7–12.
Identifiers: LCCN 2017056505| ISBN 9781508180265 (library bound) | ISBN 9781508180272 (pbk.)
Subjects: LCSH: Web site development—Vocational guidance—Juvenile literature. | Women in computer science—Juvenile literature.
Classification: LCC TK5105.888 .W36289 2019 | DDC 006.7023—dc23
LC record available at https://lccn.loc.gov/2017056505

Manufactured in the United States of America

CONTENTS

Introduction

esigner, learner, teacher, architect, investigator, supporter, challenger, communicator, tech creator. These are just some of the words that describe the responsibilities of a web developer.

As more parents buy smartphones for their children and the price of entry-level smartphones drops, companies worldwide work to attract this expanding consumer base. As the race to create the next great indispensable app heats up, we see entrepreneurs and companies creating walletless payment systems, games that interact with the environment, and fitness trackers that can measure your heart rate, blood sugar, and more.

These businesses' successes spell success for web developers, too. The Bureau of Labor Statistics (BLS) projected a 13 percent employment growth for web developers between 2016 and 2026, faster than the average growth for most jobs. As more ideas for applications are dreamed up to assist us in daily life, more web developers will be needed to create and support those apps. The creative force of female web developers will be essential to attract an increasingly diverse consumer base.

The stereotype of a tech professional is a socially awkward man who speaks in geek, but it's never a good idea to judge a career on stereotypes. In fact, women have been pioneers in the tech field from the beginning.

Ada Lovelace (1815–1852) is often credited as the first computer programmer. She was both determined and imaginative in her approach to math and science.

Ada Lovelace, an English mathematician in the 1800s, is often credited as the first person to recognize that machines could follow written instructions and be good for more than just adding and subtracting. Lovelace envisaged that "a computer can do anything that can be noted logically," according to Walter Isaacson. She worked with Charles Babbage, who is credited with creating the plans for the first mechanical computer. His designs and Lovelace's notes were read by people building the first computer a century later.

During the 1930s, female mathematicians played a key role in programming the first electronic computers. In those days, many women studied mathematics. While most went on to become teachers, others were active in research, assuming leadership positions in the mathematical community. Since the first computers were built to solve math problems, many of the first programmers were women.

Today, computers are used to solve more than mathematical problems. They are used to help journalists and academics do research, by chefs to store recipes, by stock brokers to buy and sell stocks, by artists to sell their work, by parents to learn how to take a child's temperature, and by people all over the world to connect and discuss common interests.

When you choose a career in web development, you are not making new inroads—you are reclaiming a legacy and will be shaping the face of the internet for a global audience.

Chapter one

WHAT IS A WEB DEVELOPER?

Web developers create websites using programing languages. They write detailed instructions for computers or phones about how a website should behave and look. Web developers can be found working at universities, hospitals, museums, banks, fashion houses, television stations, sports organizations, and more.

One great thing about being a web developer is that you can choose which company's work environment suits you or the type of data you enjoy working with since your job tasks are pretty much the same whether you're working for a government site collecting money for parking tickets or a shopping site selling outfits for cats.

Some web developers are entrepreneurs and work for themselves. They build and sell apps to the public. Others work as in-house or freelance web developers, building websites and apps for companies or individuals. Most web developers work as part of a team, alongside designers, marketers, and writers.

Shopping online is a valuable service for customers as it allows people to save time and energy. Businesses need web developers to maintain their online stores.

Remember, a web developer's job is never done because a website is never complete. It can always be made better, faster, easier to read, or nicer to look at.

HOW DO WEBSITES WORK ANYWAY?

A website is a collection of web pages. A web page can contain images, text, animation, video, and sound. The collection of web pages for an individual

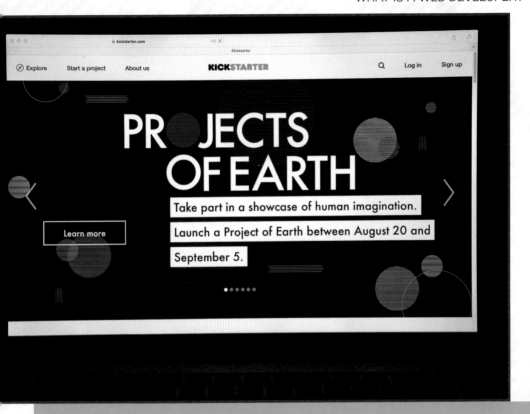

A good quality, easy-to-use website makes customers feel comfortable using a company's services. It builds trust and goodwill and will lead to increased profits.

or a company is stored on a server. Some companies have their own servers and some companies pay web hosts or service providers to store their web pages on their servers. There are servers all over the world, and they speak to each other over a network.

When you type in the address of your favorite site, your computer uses the network to make a call to the server the site is located on. The server returns the data to the computer, which displays it in the browser. Sometimes, when you go to a site and log in, the site remembers who you are and displays pictures you have uploaded or text you have saved. Websites use a database to remember who you are and things that you like. The database is like the brain of a website. When you memorize facts for a test, you store that data in your brain. When a website needs to memorize data, it stores it in a database.

Any company that wants to share information electronically with the public (such as what the weather is like in Paris) or help a user complete a task (like buying balloons for a birthday party or donating money to their favorite niece) will need a web developer.

CAREER OPTIONS FOR WEB DEVELOPERS

Web developers may be called upon to work in three main areas:

- Front end or client side. Otherwise known as the browser or the app, where the user enters input and asks the server for web pages.
- Back end or server side. Where the website is stored and serves pages or digital assets like images and video to the user when asked.
- Database. After the user has entered information, like a blog post or a selfie, the database is used to save that personalized data.

THE POWER OF DIVERSITY

Different perspectives are often helpful when you have a problem to solve. In the field of web development, there is always a problem to solve. New people are adding their code to an existing code base, users are using the site in ways the designers never expected, hackers are trying to break in—many things can go wrong. This is why companies need to build teams made up of people who tackle problems in different ways. It's the best way to prepare for the unexpected.

According to Scott E. Page, author of *The Difference: How the Power of Diversity Creates Better Groups, Firms, Schools and Societies* and *The Diversity Bonus: How Great Teams Pay Off in the Knowledge Economy,*

Diverse groups of people bring to organizations more and different ways of seeing a problem and, thus, faster/better ways of solving it. [...] People from different backgrounds have varying ways of looking at problems, what I call "tools." The sum of these tools is far more powerful in organizations with diversity than in ones where everyone has gone to the same schools, been trained in the same mold, and thinks in almost identical ways.

When you choose a career in web development, remember that your background and the ways in which you differ from your coworkers makes you a valuable employee to any company.

FRONT-END WEB DEVELOPERS

Everything a user sees in the browser is a mix of HTML, CSS, and JavaScript. A front-end web developer specializes in client-side or browser-side coding. She uses HTML to write the structure of the web page, CSS to add color and style, and JavaScript to interact with the user without checking in with the server. For example, when you fill out a form to log in to your favorite social media site, JavaScript is used to make sure you enter an email address in the email field and a password in the password field.

BACK-END WEB DEVELOPERS

A back-end web developer specializes in server-side coding. She typically works with languages such as PHP, Perl, Ruby, and MySQL to interact with the database to pull, save, and change data that users have shared with the site via a web browser. This code is not something the user can see or directly interact with.

FULL-STACK WEB DEVELOPERS

A developer who knows how to code in both front-end and back-end languages is called a full-stack web developer. Unless you have superpowers, a full-stack developer is a Jill of all trades and a master of none. A full-stack developer's job involves more learning on the job, as you have to maintain a knowledge of both front-end and back-end programming skills.

```
-- Struttura della tabella
--
CREATE TABLE IF NOT EXISTS `wp_ngg_pictures` (
 `pid` bigint(20) NOT NULL AUTO_INCREMENT,
 `image_slug` varchar(255) NOT NULL,
 `post_id` bigint(20) NOT NULL DEFAULT '0',
 `galleryid` bigint(20) NOT NULL DEFAULT '0',
 `filename` varchar(255) NOT NULL,
 `description` mediumtext,
 `alttext` mediumtext,
 `imagedate` datetime NOT NULL DEFAULT '0000-00-00 00:00
 `exclude` tinyint(4) DEFAULT '0',
 `sortorder` bigint(20) NOT NULL DEFAULT '0',
 `meta_data` longtext,
 `extras_post_id` bigint(20) NOT NULL DEFAULT '0',
 `updated_at` bigint(20) DEFAULT NULL,
 PRIMARY KEY (`pid`),
 KEY `post_id` (`post_id`),
 KEY `extras_post_id_key` (`extras_post_id`)
) ENGINE=MyISAM DEFAULT CHARSET=utf8 AUTO_INCR
-- in uso (#1142 - SELECT
```

A database is just like a book or website, except it is made up of different tables with content instead of pages with text. Developers use code to write the tables.

PROJECT MANAGERS

A project manager coordinates all phases of a web-development project. A project manager with a technical background will be able to help to turn the client's idea into words to help the web developer create the website that the client wants. A project manager understands the client's needs and the developer's needs and creates a timeframe for transforming the idea into a finished website or a section of a website.

When you learn a new language, you gain a window of insight into another culture. Without knowledge of the language, certain aspects of that culture are out of your reach. Similarly, when you learn a programming language, you gain a deeper understanding of the technology that is weaved into our contemporary lifestyles. As a web developer, you can make a living using these languages to create resources that inform and entertain millions of people around the world.

Chapter two

BECOMING A WEB DEVELOPER

You can teach yourself to code online, but the day-to-day tasks of a web developer involve more than just coding. Most web developers have at least an associate's degree in web design or a related field, and many also have a bachelor's degree. A formal education will not only help you learn the technical skills needed to be a web developer, but will also prepare you to complete projects as part of a team and help you understand different aspects of the internet and web development. This will give you an edge when you are ready to look for a job.

LEARN ABOUT THE INTERNET

A web developer should understand how the internet works and the current web standards, as outlined by the World Wide Web Consortium (WC3). The WC3 is an international community whose goal is to keep all coders on the same page. When a new word is added to a web development programming language,

Tim Berners-Lee, inventor of the World Wide Web, continues to work with politicians and web companies to fulfill his vision of the web as a free and open tool that serves everyone.

this organization will help approve it. The WC3's website, w3.org/developers, has great resources to help web developers write high quality and clean code, and to understand the importance of doing so. There are free tools to help you check if your code is written well and opportunities to join the community and give your feedback.

Designers might use Adobe Dreamweaver or Microsoft Word to build simple specs. A developer is expected to code in an advanced text editor like

Sublime, Notepad++, or an Integrated Development Environment (IDE) like PHPStorm. These programs help you follow coding standards and many offer look-up features and tips. This will help you troubleshoot and code more efficiently, as well as read and understand other people's code more quickly.

LEARNING TO CODE

Whether or not you're getting a degree in computer science or a related field, there are plenty of other ways you can learn to code. Many libraries offer free classes in basic HTML and CSS. There are also online courses such as the Odin Project and Code Avengers. Many online courses give you the flexibility of learning at your own pace, but you have to be diligent and follow through with the work.

There are some books that have tests at the end of each chapter to help you learn. Some good ones to try are *PHP and MySQL Web Development: A Beginner's Guide*, by Marty Matthews, or *HTML5 and CSS3 for Beginners: Your Guide to Easily Learn HTML5 & CSS3 Programming in 7 Days*, by iCode Academy. If you choose to learn coding from a book, you will need to read more than just one book. You may also choose to learn from a database such as SQLzoo.net.

Before you take a structured course in coding, read a basic beginner book or watch a basic beginner video. This is a great way to get a sense of the basics of what you will learn before you take the course. It will help you follow along with the teacher and ask any questions about things you'd like to know more about.

A typical developer's day involves coding, creativity, and communication. Being able to communicate in a simple and understandable manner is a valuable skill.

TAKE IT OUT OF THE CLASSROOM

Once you know the basics, take your new skills out of the classroom and the books. Practice what you have learned by creating a real website or app. You can attend hackathons and meet other techies or form a group to complete a real coding project. Is there a hobby you are passionate about? A cause you'd like to contribute to? Build your own app or website for something or someone that you love.

KNOW YOUR LEARNING STYLE

Learning one programming language can seem intimidating enough, but any aspiring web developer needs to learn a few coding languages. This may seem overwhelming. You can tackle this by understanding your learning style.

Many sites offer free tests to help you find the best way to understand new information. There's a good one on EducationPlanner.org, a public service project of the Pennsylvania Higher Education Assistance Agency: http://www.educationplanner.org/students/self-assessments/learning-styles-quiz.shtml.

Educators Neil Fleming and Colleen Mills developed a sensory-based system that divides people into five types of learners. The acronym VARK is used to describe four basic modes of learning:
V: Visual Learners—learn best via images, maps, graphs, etc.;
A: Auditory Learners—learn predominately via listening and talking;
R: Reading and Writing Learners—learn via reading and note taking;
K: Kinesthetic Learners—learn by activity and trying things.

When you understand your learning style, you can develop ways to study that help you remember information. You can learn how to become more involved in class and ask questions so that you will better understand what the teacher is saying. This makes learning technical subjects more fun. It will also help you figure out the best way to learn coding.

SOFT SKILLS

A successful web developer needs to develop both hard and soft skills. Hard skills are the basic technical skills you need to do the job. Soft skills are also known as people skills. For example, since web developers are often called upon to explain technical issues to a nontechnical crowd, they need to have good listening skills to understand their client's needs. They also need to be patient, methodical, and curious when working with code and have the ability to work with all types of people.

EMPLOYEE, FREELANCER, OR SELF-EMPLOYED?

Do you want to work as part of a large team at a company, or do you want to be a freelancer? If you're part of a large team, you will likely work on just one slice of an overall pie, so you may want to focus on developing either your front-end languages or your back-end skills to get yourself hired. If you are working on a small team or as a freelancer, you're likely to need the broader knowledge of a full-stack developer. And if you work for yourself, you'll need to have abilities in other areas, such as understanding the legal requirements of working with clients, marketing yourself, and managing finances to keep track of your business.

As a freelancer, you are your own boss. You will be running your business from the ground up, but there are organizations that offer support, such as the Freelancers Union.

JOB OUTLOOK

According to the Bureau of Labor Statistics, employment of web developers was expected to grow 13 percent from 2016 to 2026. This is faster than the average for all jobs. Demand is likely to be driven by the increasing popularity of mobile devices and e-commerce. Aspiring web developers should keep a close eye on advances in technology to stay ahead of the curve and make sure their skills are marketable in a rapidly changing industry.

Chapter three

FRONT-END WEB DEVELOPERS

A front-end web developer is responsible for making sure a website looks professional and appears the same across all browsers and devices, so she should have an eye for detail. A front-end web developer's day-to-day work involves implementing the layout of images, text, and other media on a web page. She will also have to code a responsive page. A responsive page responds to user manipulation, like resizing the browser or viewing it on a mobile or desktop device, while still making sure all the content is readable and accessible by the user. A front-end web developer checks in with the client to make sure they like the colors and placement of the images and tests the page on multiple browsers and devices.

A front-end developer needs to know what fonts are and how to change their size, weight, or style, how to use a photo-editing program, and how to code for people who have special needs—for example, not everyone can see colors or view small text. Front-end developers play an important role in making the web accessible and enjoyable for all.

If computer science is something you are passionate about, your persistence, hard work, and hours of study will be rewarded with a good salary.

PROGRAMMING LANGUAGES

JavaScript, HTML, and CSS are three of the most popular programming languages that front-end web developers work with. Each has its own part to play to make a website work.

HTML is used to create the default structure of a page. A developer will use HTML to create containers on the page to hold the website content. Will an image display at the top of the page or at the bottom? Will there be a left sidebar or a right sidebar or both? HTML answers these questions for the browser.

CSS is used to make that structure visible and user friendly. It can be used to add colors. Do you want the page to be all red with white text? You

As a web developer, the websites you create are limited only by your own imagination. CSS and JavaScript are the tools you use to make your ideas become a reality on the screen.

would use CSS to make this happen. Do you want your users to see a unicorn leaping over a rainbow when they scroll to the bottom of the page? CSS can make those dreams come true!

JavaScript makes a website like a choose-your-own-adventure book. If you want a cookie monster to pop up and say hi when a user clicks on an image of a chocolate chip cookie, you would use JavaScript to make that happen. JavaScript will help you implement concepts that involve user actions and results—"If a user does this, then that happens."

MEET DOROTHY VAUGHAN, "HUMAN COMPUTER"

"Human computer" Dorothy Vaughan was born in 1910 and earned a bachelor's degree in mathematics in 1929. She was hired as a mathematician for the National Aeronautics and Space Administration (NASA) in 1943 and went on to become the organization's first African American supervisor.

During her time at NASA, Vaughan contributed to the Scout Launch Vehicle Program. According to NASA, "Those who have worked on the Scout program have made a unique contribution to the US space program. They have created a launch vehicle system that set a standard for simplicity, productivity and reliability. They did it by establishing uncompromising standards of exactness and by an unwavering pursuit of excellence."

(continued on the next page)

(continued from the previous page)

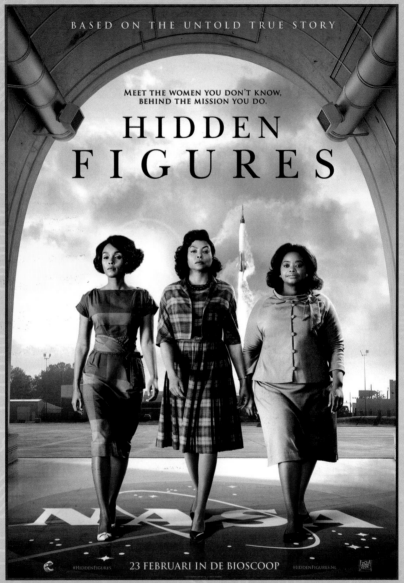

Dorothy Vaughan is played by Octavia Spencer (*right*) in the movie *Hidden Figures*, which sheds new light on the achievements of black female mathematicians.

Vaughan also became an expert FORTRAN programmer. "FORTRAN" is short for "FORmula TRANslation" and was designed to allow easy translation of math formulas into code. It is one of the oldest programming languages and is still widely used today. During her tenure at NASA, Vaughan was a steadfast advocate for equal pay for women.

Vaughan retired from NASA in 1971, after twenty-eight years of service. Her story is represented in the 2016 movie *Hidden Figures*, about the African American female mathematicians who worked for NASA during the space race.

SOFT SKILLS

In additional to having the technical skills for the job, front-end web developers should work on the soft skills of critical thinking and active listening. These skills will contribute to a productive career.

Critical thinking means having the ability to distance your emotions when you are trying to figure out a problem. Successful developers work to establish and verify facts, weigh the pros and cons of different approaches, and know how to let go of a solution if it's not working. You can work on improving your critical-thinking skills in a number of ways, including fun activities, such as doing jigsaw puzzles, making up your own recipe, gardening, or any activity where you have to observe and modify your actions based on what you learn.

Successful front-end developers also have strong active listening skills. This means the ability to give someone your full attention when that person is speaking, rather than thinking about what you are planning to say. It means staying in the moment and asking relevant questions. A skilled web developer needs to be able to have productive meetings with clients and coworkers and understand everyone's needs. One fun way to improve your active listening skills is improvisational acting, which requires you to pay close attention to the whole group.

JOB PREPARATION AND OUTLOOK

Most front-end web developers have at least an associate's degree in web design or graphic design, but the educational requirements vary depending on the type of company you work for. You'll always need to learn the basic languages, but in addition you may wish to take courses in graphic design, media production, or user interface design, depending on your interests and aspirations.

Outside of college, you can learn front-end skills through online tutorials, take a course at a private technical school (the International Web Association has a list of instructor-led, certified courses), or learn from online videos, then obtain a certification. Employers will want proof that you know a skill, so getting certified is always a good idea.

When it's time to apply for jobs, employers will want proof of your abilities. That's why it's a good idea to get certified every time you learn a new skill.

In general, the future looks bright for front-end web developers. As people expect websites to be more visually pleasing and easier to use, front-end developers will be needed to build and maintain those websites. Many front-end developer languages are also being used to build mobile applications. This puts the front-end developer at the front of the pack when it comes to being able to work with the newest technologies. Many front-end web developers move on to become senior web developers or project managers—positions that offer a salary boost.

Chapter four

BACK-END WEB DEVELOPERS

ack-end web developers are concerned with function. They need to have an understanding of the business functions of the site. For example, any site in the business of selling clown props will need a shopping cart. Back-end web developers help users add purchases to the cart, add up the total payment, and provide a secure way for the user to pay. They also create feedback for users who make mistakes, such as entering in the wrong credit card number. Where a front-end developer codes the look of a message (e.g., red with large font), the back-end developer provides the text of the message in response to user input.

Successful front-end and back-end developers share many of the same traits. They are good at problem solving, pay attention to detail, have great communication skills, and are good at working on a team. Back-end developers have more freedom in deciding how they want to build their code to solve a problem and will more often check in with other web developers to make sure they are on the right track.

Back-end code connects all the services that kick into gear after a customer hits the buy button: verifying credit cards, notifying the warehouse, and contacting the shipping company.

A BACK-END DEVELOPER'S DAY-TO-DAY WORK

Many back-end developers maintain and support content management systems (CMSs). A CMS is a piece of software that is used to write and save the site content, as well as upload images and other site media. WordPress and Drupal are popular examples of CMS. A CMS will save the content on the server either in a database or on the server hard drive (file system). Sometimes hackers try to break into the database and server hard drive through a company's CMS. Web developers have to make sure their code is secure and keep up to date with the latest security threats and best practices.

A back-end developer's responsibilities can also include application programming interface (API) maintenance and creation. An API is a set of rules and directions for how a web developer can access a website's data for use in their own web-based

When you learn the rules of a coding language, it removes the mystery and allows you to see that all languages are basically translating your words into computer lingo.

application. A back-end developer can use this technology to create an app that shows shoppers a list of stores that sell strawberry ice cream based on the location of their phone, for example. Data collection companies often share the information they've gathered with other websites, such as Yelp and Foursquare, which can then use this data to recommend businesses based on the location of your phone.

PROGRAMMING LANGUAGES

If you decide to focus on back-end web development, there are many server-side languages you can learn. It's best to choose one language and learn it well. A good language to start with is PHP. PHP is "a widely-used open source general-purpose scripting language that is especially suited for web development," according to PHP.net. PHP is free to download, and you can find many free resources, videos, forums, and online tutorials to help you learn it.

A good back-end web developer will also learn about website architecture and databases. To communicate with a database, you have to learn that database's language. One of the most popular database languages is MySQL. It is also free and easily accessible. Other popular server-side languages are Ruby on Rails, Python, and Perl. In addition, it is useful to be familiar with UNIX shell scripting languages.

If you can't decide which language to focus on, the work involved in getting a bachelor's degree in computer science will give you extensive knowledge in all aspects of web development. You will learn about how hardware works and how to write software to interact with it. Getting a certification in website security or in a server technology such as Apache can be a great way to supplement your education

Apache was founded by a group of developers who got together and decided to add more features to the web server. Their updates allowed web servers to serve interactive pages.

as a back-end web developer. If you have to do the reading, you may as well formally earn a certification to boost your marketability.

SOFT SKILLS

In addition to learning these programming languages, aspiring back-end developers would do well to develop their concentration and communication skills.

Web developers are hired to write code, but they will also be required to attend regular meetings and need to be able to answer questions and concerns from project managers, clients, and other developers politely and accurately, all while churning out clean working code. You can work on your concentration skills by practicing any activity that requires you to do more than one thing at the same time. For example, in partner dancing you have to listen to music while matching your steps with your partner's steps.

Strong communication skills will help in all aspects of your life, but in your workplace, the ability to write clear and concise emails can save a lot of time. You should be able to clearly convey to managers how much time you need for a project and alert them in a timely manner to any roadblocks you encounter along the way. If you find a bug in your coworker's code, explain this kindly while acknowledging the hard work that person put in. Good communication is key to a happy workplace.

JOB OUTLOOK

Back-end developers can look forward to steady paychecks for years to come. As companies move more of their offline business functions online, the demand for back-end developers grows. Back-end developers often move on to become senior web developers, full-stack developers, or project managers. These positions all come with higher salaries.

Chapter five

FULL-STACK AND FREELANCE WEB DEVELOPERS

A full-stack web developer knows how to code in both server-side and client-side languages and is expected to understand the web stack: the software required for web development. This includes the operating system, the database, the programming language, and the web server. A freelance web developer is a professional who is self-employed and works on a contract basis for businesses or individual clients. Freelancers need to have many of the same skills as full-stack web developers.

PROGRAMMING LANGUAGES AND SKILLS

Full-stack and freelance web developers should both learn a combination of client- and server-side language, such as JavaScript, jQuery, HTML, Sass, CSS, PHP, Python, and Ruby.

Asking for feedback is a great way to keep the lines of communication open with your clients. Status updates help to keep the project on track.

They should also know how to install, maintain, and upgrade a CMS like WordPress. Aspiring full-stack and freelance developers should start with a simple CMS and study the general format used to add content to a site. Learning about internet security and how the internet works will also prove invaluable.

Full-stack and freelance web developers may also wish to learn how to use a framework like AngularJS or Yii. A framework is a software application that uses a combination of code libraries and other programming tools. It is used by web developers as a foundation to build an application on. Frameworks help you code basic tasks faster.

FREELANCING

A freelance developer should maintain an up-to-date online portfolio that highlights her skills. Freelancers need to provide clients with regular status updates. They also need to track their payments and negotiate their own contracts, so it is helpful to have some financial and legal knowledge. Many freelancers contract out for a specific number of hours since projects can often run longer than anticipated.

Joining a freelancer organization or becoming a member of a professional community that focuses on an area you want to be a specialist in will keep you inspired and informed, and it can also be a good way to find work and learn about new trends. Being a member of an organization can be a great source of support and mentorship for web developers who work on their own.

SOFT SKILLS

A large part of a web developer's career will involve troubleshooting—the ability to solve problems by using logic to narrow the possibilities. This means keeping an open mind and not making assumptions. Rock climbing is a great way to improve your problem-solving skills, as you have to hold your own body weight while assessing the best course. And there's a reason why chess has stood the test of time—it's an excellent way to refine your problem-solving techniques.

A typical web developer's job involves some form of teaching. You don't have to be an expert in a subject to teach—you just have to share your experience with someone who knows less than you. You may be the first person on the team to work with a particular software package, and you need to bring your coworkers up to speed. Freelancers may have to train their clients to use a new feature they've built. There are many ways to improve your teaching skills.

Teaching any subject is a great way to learn how to organize your thoughts. The ability to remember details while speaking is a skill that keeps successful web developers employed.

You could volunteer to help seniors use technology with confidence. You could volunteer as a museum docent. Any activity that involves knowledge sharing can help.

EDUCATION

A typical full-stack developer has a degree in computer science, which provides a foundation in mathematics, different programming languages, hardware knowledge, and an understanding of how the web and computers work. Full-stack developers and freelancers should supplement their education by obtaining certifications in front-end and back-end languages to keep them well rounded.

HEALTHY BODY AND BRAIN: TIPS FOR THE DESKBOUND TECH GIRL

Testing, troubleshooting, and creating code can take a toll on your body—and your brain. A web developer should treat her brain like an athlete treats her body, and that means maintaining a well-rounded lifestyle. There are a few simple things you can do to take care of your body and your brain. This will help you stay methodical, creative, and curious.

- Drink water. Dehydration impairs your mental performance and physical coordination even before you start to feel thirsty. You'll feel better and work smarter by drinking water throughout the day. Buy a nice water bottle to keep you inspired to stay hydrated.

- Get some time in the sun. When you take a break from work, go outside and take a walk in the sunshine. Make this part of your daily routine.
- Find time to exercise before or after work. You could ride your bike to work. You could wake up early and run. You could take an exercise class after work.
- Schedule time for family and friends. Write out your values and keep them somewhere where you'll see them every day.
- Learn meditation techniques to keep your mind limber and help you focus. Use desk stretches and a TheraBand to rejuvenate your mind and relieve stress.

Riding a bike to work or to run errands is a great way to keep your body—and your brain—healthy for work, studying, and life.

JOB OUTLOOK

Full-stack developers are in high demand and can expect a relatively high salary compared to other web developers. Many companies are reluctant to pay two developers when one full-stack developer has the ability to make front-end and back-end updates. Full-stack developers often move on to become senior web developers or project managers. While freelancer web developers can't rely on a steady paycheck, those who are savvy and know how to market themselves can charge high rates while enjoying the flexibility of not being tied to a nine-to-five schedule.

Chapter six

TECHNICAL PROJECT MANAGERS

According to Marlo Young, a project manager for the World Bank,

> If you're a tech project manager, it's not just [about] tech skills or certs like the PMP. It's also social skills. How do you get info out

Successful project managers understand what it takes to help a diverse group of people work together. Team-building skills play a crucial role.

of people, pick out the parts of the info that are relevant to person A versus person B, and get people to work together? Can you bring harmony to the people? Because the people drive the project. And organization—getting it all organized so everyone knows what's happening.

If you know the front-end and back-end languages and you think you would enjoy lots of client interaction, you like working with spreadsheets and numbers to estimate how long technical projects will take, and you follow blogs and read industry newsletters to keep up with new tech trends, you may be ready to become a project manager.

BECOMING A PROJECT MANAGER

Some technical project managers work their way up from being web developers. Many companies like to hire a manager who has technical experience and understands the project life cycle from doing it. Some project managers come from nontechnical backgrounds, though, and may have degrees in disciplines such as English, economics, or art. If you're a project manager who comes from a nontechnical background, you'll need to study up on the life cycle of a web-development project and understand the technical language of the web.

Getting a project management professional (PMP) certification from the Project Management Institute (PMI) will put you ahead of the competition, whether you've worked your way up or are coming in from another field. The PMI is also a great resource for tools to help you keep track of project deadlines, boost productivity, and address project roadblocks. There are templates and checklists available for different industries.

A technical project manager must also understand the site or application she is helping to create. She may need to jump in and do some testing to make sure the application is stable and delivers what the client has asked for. Project managers also provide technical leadership. They should be able to recognize, for example, if a project will take longer than expected and needs to be broken down into different pieces.

SOFT SKILLS

In addition to the technical skills, project managers need to be patient and have good judgment. Because they serve as go-betweens for clients and developers, they must be able to keep themselves, others, and the project as a whole on schedule. If it looks like a project is going off the rails, project managers are responsible for taking corrective action. This requires knowing how to manage stress and having a deep well of patience. Having a meditation practice can help you become more patient and manage stress. Mastering a new skill, like learning an instrument or how to break-dance, can also help you learn patience.

Project managers should have good judgment and be able to make decisions based on sound reasoning or common sense. A project manager may, after looking at facts and weighing opinions, decide

Stress can seriously affect your health and productivity. The good news is, with the right techniques, you can reduce stress and regain a feeling of control.

to cancel a project or extend a project deadline. These types of decisions may be made with the client and team or independently. Any activity that allows you to practice your leadership skills—such as choreographing a dance routine for your friends or starting a meet-up group—can help you improve your judgment.

APP ENTREPRENEURS

Do you want to become an app entrepreneur? Then start with a list of problems. Write down as many things as you can that you wish were easier to do. For example, "When it's summertime and I'd really like an ice-cream cone, I can never find the ice-cream truck." Then look at the list and circle the ones that you find the most interesting. Use your technical training to

(continued on the next page)

Dawoon Kang, who founded Coffee Meets Bagel with her sisters, attributes their success to their role models and imagination.

(continued from the previous page)

determine which problems would be possible to solve. And just like that, you are on your way to joining the app entrepreneurs of the world.

Arum, Dawoon, and Soo Kang are three sisters who founded the mobile dating app Coffee Meets Bagel in 2012. The app provides a limited list of potential dates for a user every day at noon. Users have twenty-four hours to decide whether to "like" or "pass" on a match, and they can start messaging only once they've both approved each other.

Cofounder Soo Kang explains what problem they aimed to solve with their app: "Men and women have very different approaches to dating…. We're all about giving you a meaningful connection. Most other dating services, like Tinder, are about serving up as many profiles as possible. It gets tiring. It also leads to very bad behavior on the guys' part—abusing the platform. Even [*Shark Tank's*] Barbara Corcoran mentioned it's almost insulting for a lot of women to use that kind of service."

JOB PREPARATION AND OUTLOOK

As companies rely on websites for more and more areas of their work, project managers are increasingly in demand. Project managers typically have at least a bachelor's degree, either in computer or information science, or in an unrelated field. Many technical managers also have graduate degrees.

Chapter seven

GETTING HIRED

Y ou've learned your languages, you've gotten the degree or certifications, and now you want to get a job as a web developer. Where do you start?

CREATE A PORTFOLIO

Start by creating a portfolio. A portfolio is a visual presentation of your skills. The developers who get job offers are the ones who not only learn the skills, but can also prove that they know how to use them.

Building a portfolio should be fun. Try out new technologies. Do you have a friend who is a struggling actor? You could offer to create an online portfolio for him or her. This is a great opportunity to practice your soft skills—listening, communicating well, working with nontechnical people, meeting a deadline—and your friend can then provide a reference when you need one. Or you could volunteer to build a site for your favorite local pizza place, or add a new feature to your community center or church's website. Are you hosting a game night? Invite your friends using an app that you created!

WordPress and other content management sites make it easy for users to publish their words online without having to know any CSS or HTML.

Another great way to demo your skills is to theme a template from a CMS like Drupal or WordPress, or redesign a page of a popular website. A back-end developer can add a new feature to a popular website or build a plug-in for a CMS.

A good web-development portfolio should be an honest representation of who you are. It should represent your career goals. It should also include projects that demonstrate that you know the languages for the position for which you are applying. Always be prepared for an interviewer to ask about the projects that you include in your portfolio or even to see your work. Your code doesn't have to be complex, and your app doesn't have to have thousands of downloads—the employer just wants to see your passion and determine if your goals align with theirs.

WRITE A RÉSUMÉ

Your résumé is a one-page summary of your skills, education, and experience. This is your opportunity to describe how your work impacted a client. For example, did the actor's online portfolio that you created help her book two commercials and get into grad school? You should tailor your résumé for each job you apply for. If you're applying to work for a nonprofit that focuses on educating disadvantaged youth, you might want to highlight the site updates you did for your local community center.

BUILD AN ONLINE TECH PRESENCE

Open a GitHub account and contribute to it. Save the code you are most proud of. It doesn't have to be long chunks of code; even a few lines of code count. Open an account on Stack Overflow and answer or ask a question. Contribute to open-source software. Aspiring front-end developers can create free themes, or improve existing ones. A back-end developer can create a new library or bug fix or patch an existing one. You can also write help text for a code library or write a tech blog with tips to help others learn programming.

SHOW OFF YOUR SKILLS!

- ## Earn Digital Badges

Girl scouts earn badges when they learn a new skill, such as how to start a campfire, or provide community service. Digital badges are badges anyone can earn online to prove they have learned a hard or soft skill. You can learn more about them at OpenBadges.org. Thousands of organizations around the world issue digital badges. For example, you could earn a fitness badge from the YMCA or a math badge from BuzzMath.com. You

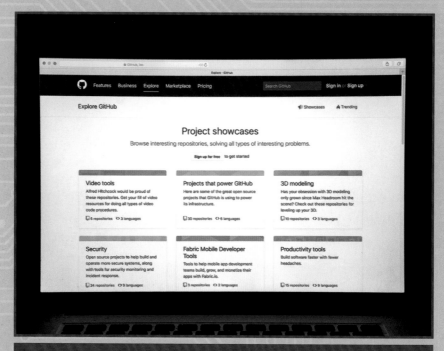

Visually presenting your coding work online is a way to demonstrate your achievements and the skills you've learned.

can display badges you've earned on blogs, websites, portfolios, social media sites, and in your email signature. See where badges have been earned around the world by checking out BadgeTheWorld.org. One great badge to start your collection is the Super Girl and the Navigator badge: http://toolness.github.io /hackasaurus-parable/navigator-badge.

- **Build Your Own Computer**

Ada Lovelace realized that machines could understand instructions by looking at drawings. You can channel your inner Ada Lovelace by building your own computer with a DIY kit! Some fun ones can be found at Piper (BuildPiper.com) and Kano (Kano.me). DIY computers are a fun way to learn how to program and understand computers from the inside out.

- **Build Your Own Mobile App**

You could also try building your own mobile app and sharing it with friends and family. App Inventor (AppInventor.org) is a great place to start.

FIND THE JOBS

You've set yourself up. Now it's time to apply for jobs. A great way to find jobs is through your social networks offline and online. Ask around and see if there are openings at places your friends or family work. Send them your portfolio and résumé to make it easier for them to refer you.

You should also read industry blogs and newsletters, such as PHP Weekly, CSS-Tricks, CodePen, PlanetMySQL, and InfoWorld. Some of these sites also have job boards, like jobs.drupal.org. Check out companies' job listings on their websites. Then go the extra step and find the name of the hiring manager so you know whom to address your cover letter to. Yes, cover letters are still important. They give you the opportunity to personalize your résumé and portfolio. Use a cover letter to describe why you'd like to work for that specific company, show off any research you've done, and explain any relevant experience.

When you apply to work at a company whose mission aligns with your values and career path, it is easier to get hired. Look around a company's website, read their mission statement, go through their blogs. Understand the place you are applying to. Then ask yourself if this company is a good fit for you. Will you grow your language skills in this position? Does the company value continuing education? Can you expand your soft skill set? Will your technical input be valued?

TRACK YOUR PROGRESS

Looking for a job takes work. Use a spreadsheet to keep track of where you've applied, the outcome, and any contacts you made there. Being consistent pays off in a job search. Make a schedule for your job search process. Set yourself a goal for how many jobs you apply for every day or every week. Doing your research and writing good cover letters takes time.

Prepare yourself for rejection. It happens to everyone, but it still hurts. Take a moment to mourn, jump up and down, scream, then get back to work. Think of every job you don't get as a learning experience. Use your job search as an opportunity to improve upon that essential developer skill of persistence. You keep applying until you get an interview. You keep interviewing until you get a job offer.

ACE THE INTERVIEW

Acing an interview doesn't start when the interview starts. You need to spend time preparing. If you've kept a good spreadsheet, you'll have some notes from your research. Reread them and write down any questions you have for the interviewer. Print a few copies of your résumé to take with you and refresh yourself about what you wrote in your cover letter. Be prepared to talk about projects in your portfolio, résumé, and GitHub work if you have done any.

Map out how long it takes to get to the interview location and plan on arriving a few minutes early. You may get lost, have a tough time finding parking, or need to sign in with security. It's always better to have extra time on your hands. It will leave you looking relaxed and collected when you arrive for your interview.

Interviews can be scary, but it helps to remember two things:

1. The interviewer wants you to be a candidate he or she can hand an offer to. This position is open for a reason. The company needs someone to do it and they want it filled.

Interview skills are learned, and they improve the more you practice. Above all else, be authentic when communicating your skills and passion.

2. This interview is about you. If you have been honest and truthful in your résumé, portfolio, and online presence, then you will merely be providing more detail about who you are.

You may also be asked to do a technical interview. This could be in the form of a physical test or by asking you to go into the technical details of what you've done. This varies widely by company. You should certainly feel free to ask ahead of time what the interview format will be. You may not get an answer, but there is no shame in asking. In any case, you should always do your research, know yourself, come prepared, and show your passion for web development.

After the interview, demonstrate your people skills and written communication skills with a thank-you email. Make sure to get the names and email addresses of the people you met with and thank them for taking the time to consider you for the job. Even if you don't think you're going to get the job, you should always try your best to make a good impression—you never know when another position may open up at that company.

Chapter eight

THE LEARNING NEVER ENDS

*P*ioneering computer scientist Grace Hopper once said, "Humans are allergic to change. They love to say, 'We've always done it this way.' I try to fight that. That's why I have a clock on my wall that runs counter-clockwise."

Hopper used a clock to remind her to always strive to improve. Learning to work with change is a life skill everyone should have, but web developers, in particular, need to feel comfortable with learning new skills. Advances in technology often provide web developers with concrete ways to improve their skills by introducing a new language or a reason to use existing languages in a new way.

When you choose to pursue a career as a web developer, expect to continue to grow your hard skills by learning new programming languages and keeping up with tech trends. What will you put on your wall to remind you that change is coming?

MAKE A DIFFERENCE

At the age of seventeen, Brittany Wenger was a grand prize winner of the Google Science Fair Award

Brittany Wenger achieved success by using the skills she learned in school to address a problem she saw in her life. When you care about your work, you are more likely to excel.

with her breast cancer diagnosis app. The app is able to detect 99 percent of cancer cases. Wenger got the idea to create this app by watching the impact of her cousin's breast cancer diagnosis. She was able to use her coding skills to solve a problem that was very personal to her.

You don't have to create an app that saves lives to have a successful web career, but you should find work where you use your skills solving problems that interest you or work for a company whose mission you support. This is how you will keep your passion alive.

No matter what you do, you have to love doing it. You don't have to be a math genius, have the highest IQ, or use all the technical terms you know while chatting with friends to have a successful career as a web developer. You have to be persistent and curious to learn your first programming language. And you have to learn ways to stay passionate to make web development a long-term career.

INVEST IN YOURSELF

When you invest in yourself, it's like opening a savings account. Money in your savings account is not money you spend right away. When you find yourself broke, would you rather ask for loans, sell your favorite item, or make a withdrawal from your savings account? Investing in yourself is like creating a freedom fund.

- **Find a coach or mentor**—somebody to help you keep track of your goals. Have you lost your motivation? Do you find yourself watching a *Sharknado* marathon instead of attending that improv class you were thinking of going to or reading the headlines on Techcrunch.com? When you encounter problems in your career, you will need a support system. A mentor can keep you on track and provide that support. You could start by checking out CodeMentor.
- **Start or contribute to a savings account regularly**. Pay your bills. Live simply if you have to until you reach your goal. A small step with a big impact is to make your own lunch instead of buying it every day. There are apps like

Mint that help you save, starting with just pennies a day. Being financially stable will empower you to choose work that interests you.

- **Start a work journal.** Check in daily or weekly. What successes have you had? What was the project you most enjoyed? How can you improve? What questions do you need to answer? What have you learned? Journaling can help you to understand your strengths and weaknesses, which in turn helps you to interview better, be a better team player, and make a clear plan for your continuing education.

Taking the time out to reflect reduces stress and keeps you on track. Try using a pen and paper to write about your day as a way to slow down.

CREATE COMMUNITY

After you learn the basic skills it takes to do your job, think about joining or creating a community that inspires you to learn, share, and give back. Meet other web developers offline. Different learning happens when you speak to people face to face. Meetup.com is a great resource to find local developer events like workshops, study groups, and seminars. If you don't find one that works for you, create your own. Being active in a tech community also helps with your communication skills, which in turn makes you better at your job.

Developers often have to solve similar problems, and the web development profession grows when developers share knowledge. You can often find the solution to a common problem by searching the internet and reading the technical forums. You can contribute to the community by simply asking questions, joining the technical discussions, or solving the problems posed by your fellow developers. You do not have to be an expert to join these online communities. Every day that you program, you are solving problems. By participating in these forums, you are just sharing what you learn in your daily life.

All web developers benefit when more diverse voices contribute to the community. Seek out and surround yourself with positive role models. Ask when you don't understand. Make sure your opinion is heard. Speak even if you aren't sure if you're right. It's better to be strong and wrong than silent.

Many technical innovations, apps, and companies have been founded by teams. Use your community to teach, learn, share, and connect.

And don't forget that who you are—your background and your values—combined with your technical skills makes you a valuable asset to any community. Hold on to this work-life balance to maintain your passion while creating a bigger and better internet for all.

Glossary

APP A web application. Apps are built for mobile and tablet devices. Users must go to an app store to download and install the application to their devices.

APPLICATION PROGRAMMING INTERFACE (API) A set of rules and directions for how a web developer can access a website's data for use in her own web-based application.

BACK-END DEVELOPER A programmer who uses server-side languages to code features that interact with the database or server.

CERTIFICATION A document that is given to a person by a respected authority. It usually requires an exam to obtain and can be used as proof of a certain skill.

CLIENT-SIDE LANGUAGES Languages that are used in the browser and decide how content displays or interacts with the user without connecting to the server or database.

CODE LIBRARIES Reusable pieces of code that perform a specific task, such as calculating a tip, or drawing a circle. Each language has its own set of libraries that programmers use to assist with coding.

CONTENT MANAGEMENT SYSTEM (CMS) A software application used to create, edit, and publish content to a website.

DATABASE A software application that lives on the server and can store data for millions of users. It has its own language that can be used to save, search, and retrieve the data stored within.

ENTREPRENEUR A person who has an idea to solve a problem, makes a plan, takes the risk, and starts a business.

FRAMEWORK A software application that uses a combination of code libraries and other programming tools, which programmers can use as a foundation and guide to build an application.

FREELANCER A person who is self-employed and works on a contract basis for businesses or solo clients.

FRONT-END DEVELOPER A programmer who uses client-side languages to code features that interact with the browser and website display.

FULL-STACK DEVELOPER A programmer who can code in server-side and client-side languages and is knowledgeable about all areas of the web stack.

HACKER A programmer who breaks into computer systems, such as a website database or company email server, to steal, alter, destroy, or hold data hostage. A hacker can also describe a programmer who can write creative code when a temporary quick fix is needed to solve a technical problem.

HARD SKILLS The basic computer and language skills

needed to do a job.

INTERNET A large group of connected computers and other electronic devices that share data.

OPEN-SOURCE SOFTWARE Any software application certified by the Open Source Initiative (OSI). This software makes its source code available.

PORTFOLIO A visual summary of a person's skills and accomplishments.

SERVER-SIDE LANGUAGES Languages a programmer uses to write code on the server. The server sends web content to the browser. Back-end code changes the data or builds a page for display before it can be seen by the user.

SOFT SKILLS Skills that enable a person to work well with other people, such as active listening and communication skills.

WEBSITE A collection of web pages, stored on a web server.

WEB STACK The software required for web development. This includes the operating system, the database, a programming language, and the web server.

Girl Develop It
1732 1st Avenue, #24681
New York, NY, 10128
Website: https://www.girldevelopit.com
Facebook and Twitter: @girldevelopit
Girl Develop It is a nonprofit organization that
    provides affordable programs for adult women
    interested in learning web and software
    development in a judgment-free environment.

Girls Who Code
28 W 23rd Street, Floor 4
New York, NY 10010
Website: https://www.girlswhocode.com
Facebook, Twitter, and Instagram: @GirlsWhoCode
Girls Who Code is a nonprofit organization founded
    with a single mission: to close the gender gap
    in technology. It offers after-school clubs and
    summer immersion programs nationwide for
    sixth- to twelfth-grade girls to explore coding in
    a fun and friendly environment.

Graphic Designers of Canada (GDC)
Arts Court, 2 Daly Avenue,
Ottawa, Ontario, K1N 6E2
Canada
Website: https://gdc.design
Facebook and Twitter: @GDCNational
GDC is a member-based organization of design
    professionals, educators, administrators,

students, and affiliates in communications, marketing, media, and design-related fields.

National Center for Women & Information Technology (NCWIT)
University of Colorado
Campus Box 417 UCB
Boulder, CO 80309
Website https://www.ncwit.org
Facebook and Twitter: @ncwit
NCWIT is a nonprofit organization that convenes, equips, and unites change-leader organizations to increase the meaningful participation of all women—at the intersections of race, ethnicity, class, age, sexual orientation, and disability status—in the influential field of computing, particularly in terms of innovation and development.

Society of Internet Professionals (SIP)
IP, 120 Carlton Street, Suite 305
Toronto, ON, M5A 4K2
Canada
Website: http://www.sipgroup.org
Twitter: @sipgroup
The Society of Internet Professionals is a nonprofit, membership-based organization representing the interests of internet professionals.

Women in Communications and Technology (WCT)
7 Bayview Road
Ottawa, ON, K1Y 2C5
Canada
Website: https://www.wct-fct.com/en
Facebook: @womenincommunicationsandtechnology
Twitter: @wctfct
Women in Communications and Technology
    empowers women in broadcasting, cable,
    telecommunications, digital media, and technology
    to achieve professional success, to aim higher, and
    to be recognized for their achievements.

World Organization of Webmasters (WOW)
PO Box 584
Washington, IL 61571
Website: http://webprofessionals.org
Facebook: @webprofessionals
Twitter: @WebProMinute
The World Organization of Webmasters is a
    nonprofit professional association dedicated to
    the support of individuals and organizations who
    create, manage, or market websites.

For Further Reading

Briggs, Jason R. *Python for Kids: A Playful Introduction to Programming*. San Francisco, CA: No Starch Press, 2012.

Hayes, Amy. *Ada Lovelace: First Computer Programmer*. New York, NY: Rosen Publishing, 2017.

Gonzales, Andrea and Sophie Houser. *Girl Code: Gaming, Going Viral, and Getting It Done*. New York, NY: HarperCollins, 2017.

iCode Academy. *HTML5 & CSS3 For Beginners: Your Guide to Easily Learn HTML5 & CSS3 Programming in 7 Days*. Pasig, Phillipines: iCodeAcademy, 2017.

iCode Academy. *PHP for Beginners: Your Guide to Easily Learn PHP In 7 Days*. Pasig, Phillipines: iCodeAcademy, 2017.

Ignotofsky, Rachel. *Women in Science: 50 Fearless Pioneers Who Changed the World*. Emeryville, CA: Ten Speed Press, 2016.

La Bella, Laura. *How Do I Use a Database?* New York, NY: Rosen Publishing, 2015.

Lengstorf, Jason, and Thomas Blom Hansen. *PHP for Absolute Beginners*. New York, NY: Apress, 2014.

Matthews, Marty. *PHP and MySQL Web Development: A Beginner's* Guide. New York, NY: McGraw-Hill Education, 2014.

Morgan, Nick. *JavaScript for Kids: A Playful Introduction to Programming*. San Francisco, CA: No Starch Press, 2014.

Niver, Heather Moore. *Getting to Know Ruby* (Code Power). New York, NY: Rosen Publishing, 2014.

Shetterly, Margaret Lee. *Hidden Figures.* Young Readers' ed. New York, NY: HarperCollins, 2016.

Sonmez, John. *Soft Skills: The Software Developer's Life Manual.* Greenwich, CT: Manning Publications, 2014.

Swaby, Rachel. *Headstrong: 52 Women Who Changed Science—and the World.* New York, NY: Broadway Books, 2015.

Bibliography

Borel, Brooke. "This College Freshman Is a Cancer Detective: A Q&A with Brittany Wenger." Ideas .TED.com, December 12, 2013. https://ideas.ted .com/brittany-wenger-cancer-research.

Bureau of Labor Statistics. "Occupational Outlook Handbook: Web Developers." Retrieved October 30, 2017. https://www.bls.gov/ooh/computer-and -information-technology/web-developers.htm.

Drupal Association. "DrupalCon New Orleans 2016: Community Keynote: Michael Schmid." YouTube, video posted May 12, 2016. https://www .youtube.com/watch?v=ZA95tpXUIos.

Ferdig, Richard, and Kristine Pytash. "There's a Badge for That." Tech & Learning, February 26, 2014. http://www.techlearning.com/news/0002 /theres-a-badge-for-that/63725.

Guido, Marcus. "How Hobbies Improve Performance at Work." Sandglaz, October 13, 2014. http://blog.sandglaz.com/hobbies-can -improve-performance-at-work.

Isaacson, Walter. *The Innovators: How a Group of Inventors, Hackers, Geniuses, and Geeks Created the Digital Revolution.* New York, NY: Simon & Schuster, 2014.

Murray, Margaret A. M. *Women Becoming Mathematicians: Creating a Professional Identity in Post-World War II America.* Cambridge, MA: MIT Press, 2001.

National Center for O*NET Development. "Summary Report for 15-1134.00-Web Developers." O*NET

OnLine. Retrieved October 30, 2017. https://
www.onetonline.org/link/summary/15-1134.00.

Page, Scott E. *The Diversity Bonus: How Great
Teams Pay Off in the Knowledge Industry.*
Princeton, NJ: Princeton University Press, 2017.

Sydell, Laura. "The Forgotten Female Programmers
Who Created Modern Tech." National Public
Radio, October 6, 2014. https://www.npr.org
/sections/alltechconsidered/2014/10
/06/345799830/the-forgotten-female
-programmers-who-created-modern-tech.

Taylor, Jordyn. "Why Did These Dating App
Founders Turn Down the Largest Offer in 'Shark
Tank' History?" *Observer*, January 13, 2015
http://observer.com/2015/01/why-did-these
-dating-app-founders-turn-down-the-largest
-offer-in-shark-tank-history.

Varshneya, Rahul. "A Step-by-Step Guide to
Building Your First Mobile App." *Entrepreneur*,
January 31, 2014. https://www.entrepreneur
.com/article/231145.

Walravens, Samantha, and Heather Cabot. "How
This Sister-Run Business Is Changing the Dating
Game." *Forbes*, February 13, 2017. https://www
.forbes.com/sites/geekgirlrising/2017/02/13
/how-this-sister-run-business-is-changing-the
-dating-game/#7ce9669f4086.

Young, Marlo (project manager, World Bank).
Interview with the author, September 25, 2017.

Index

ABOUT THE AUTHOR

Maryam Washington has a degree in computer science from Smith College and has been coding software applications for over twenty years. She has been doing the web development project life cycle flow for almost ten years. Washington lives in New York City, loves to read, and has taken writing, art, singing, dance, yoga, and circus classes to keep up a work-life balance. She surrounds herself with women who share and inspire her to maintain her passion for coding in this male-dominated field.

PHOTO CREDITS